I0017610

The ultimate quick guide for speeding up your pc

Go faster! Expert tips for top pc performances

*Many thanks to all the people
I've meet during these years: teachers,
technicians, IT and network engineers, because without their
precious teachings and suggestions, this book
wouldn't have been made.*

Acknowledgements

Thanks to my family and friends, for having always been present.

The purpose of this book is to provide a resource for you when you are wondering how to do something better, how to do it more easily, or even how to do it at all.
The steps you'll find are very specific and, hopefully, quite complete.
Enjoy the reading!

R.Ruggiu

Limit of Liability/Disclaimer of Warranty

The author make no representations or warranties with respect to the accuracy or completeness of the contents of this work and specifically disclaim all warranties, including without limitation warranties of fitness for a particular purpose.
The advice and strategies contained herein may not be suitable for every situation.
This work is sold with the understanding that the publisher is not engaged in rendering legal, accounting, or other professional services.
If professional assistance is required, the services of a competent professional person should be sought.
The author shall not be liable for damages arising hereform.
The fact that an organisation is referred to in this work as a citation and/or a potential source of further information does not mean that the author endorses the information the organization may provide or recommendations it may make.
Further, readers should be aware that the author shall not be liable for damages arising hereform.

Trademarks: all the trademarks in this book are the property of their respective owners. The author is not associated with any product or or vendor mentioned in this book.

Introduction

Dear Reader,
this book is meant to speed up your pc with top performances, or restore it as quickly as possible with the least expense!
There is no particular order to the topics in this book so you can jump to any chapter without having read the proceeding ones.
To get started, I recommend that you take a look at the table of contents and decide which question you'd like answered first.
Turn the appropriate page and off you go!

Contents

Disclaimer: breaking through the performances barrier to go beyond the official specs and modifying internal components, could make you loose the warranty.

…Before starting the journey, let's have a cup of coffee!

Chapter I
Expand PC capabilities with peripherals
Hardware overview

A peripheral is a device that expands the basic computer system, providing it with capabilities specific to your needs.

These devices are installed internally or externally wired or wireless, the variety is rich.

Peripherals can be added to any computer, but only the desktop model offers internal expansion.

As with everything in the computer universe, hardware works with software to get things accomplished.

If you plan on opening up the computer to add or remove internal components, you may need a standard Phillips head screwdriver.

Finally you will need the peripherals you want to add to your computer system.

Some components require plenty of patience to install.

Console Tour
Exploring inside the case

Let's start with the "box" of the computer. The main part of the computer system is known as the console.

The console is the principal part of the computer system. Peripherals are connected to the console to complete the computer system.

Some peripherals are strictly necessary, such as the computer monitor or the keyboard.

There are several kinds of consoles, such as desktops, mini-tower, the all in one solution based on a console inside the monitor and the laptops.

Inside the console, you find three important items: the motherboard, the mass storage and the power supply.

The motherboard is the computer's main circuitry board.

It connects and "hosts" many important elements in the computer system.

The first one is the processor or cpu, for central processing unit.

Stored on the motherboard there is also the computer's chip set, once was called Bios (basic input output system).

The chip set handles a lot of operations, such as networking, video output and so on.

The motherboard hosts also the computer memory, or RAM.

Memory cards are also called Sims or Dims, are inserted into the motherboard.

You'll find also display adapter cards in one of the slots inside the motherboard, in order to improve video quality performances.

Finally the motherboard is equipped with various connectors.

These connectors interacts with others parts of the system (both internal and external).

One of this connectors goes to the mass storage device a hard drive (HDD) or a solid state drive (SSD).

The console could house many internal storage devices if one or more drive cages are available.

Another mass storage option   is an optical drive. Nowadays this kind of peripheral is not used such as once were.

Going on, the console hosts a power supply. The tasks of the power supply is to give power to the system.

The second task of the power supply is to keep the console cooled through a fan.

The Cpu also and sometimes graphic cards hosts cooling fans in order to extract and dissipate heat.

The console hosts some input and output panels (or IO panels).

These panels are used to connect input and output devices that connect to the motherboard.

Usually the can find the IO panel in the back of the PC tower.

It provides USB ports, network port (RJ45), audio and video ports, etc.

Usually a video port is available in the back of the pc, but sometimes you can find a second one from the display adapter card.

You can find another IO panel in front of the pc, wich hosts some USB ports, or other ports in order to easily attach devices such as USB external HHD, pen drive, or headsets.

Input and output peripherals

Peripherals devices deal with input and output and the can be either inside or outside the console.

But most often they're outside.

Even if the peripheral is inside the console, it's still considered a peripheral in a traditional sense.

The most basic of these peripherals are what's called standard input and standard output devices.

The standard input device in a computer, is the keyboard. The standard output device is the monitor.

Both these devices are considered peripherals, whether they're separate from the console, as with most desktop PCs, or integrated into the console, as they are in a laptop or even a all-in-one PC.

Other output devices are speakers and/or headphones.

The printer is also considered as output device, and it could even include a fax machine integrated into the printer's hardware (maybe the oldest ones).

Another output device would be a second monitor or a projector to a laptop.

That's also an output device, and it's a peripheral.

Other common input peripherals would include a mouse or a pointing device.

It doesn't necessarily need to be a mouse.

A microphone is another input device; it could also be included in a headset, so it's an input/output devices (the speakers on the headset are output).

The scanner, is considered an input device. It may be part of the printer, so the printer is both an output and an input device.

A webcam is also an input peripheral, and it could be integrated in the monitor too.

Another input device is a gamepad or a joystick.

And there are many other peripherals out there.

A lot of peripherals provide both input and output; the list includes external storage such as an external hard drive or a media card or a thumb drive.

The network is also considered a peripheral that provides both input and output.

The modem provides also input and output.

Touchscreen monitor is considered input and output.

Again, these peripherals can be integrated into the console or can be a part of external devices.

Chapter II
Improving performances

If you're going to improve the performances of your pc (both 5/6 years old or brand new one) you can proceed as described in this chapter.

Without upsetting too much your machine, you can add some RAM and swap your HDD with a more performance one.

In order to buy the right RAM modules for your pc, you must check the motherboard specs to see how much RAM you can add to get the maximum performances.

Regarding the HDD, you can swap your standard HDD with an SSD one (this swap, will speed up your computer while reading or writing data, and during the normal use).

Everything mentioned above, is a good solution for a laptop or a desktop pc.

You could obviously go on modifying your computer, but I would suggest not going on with further improvements in order to maintain a good value for money. Changing the graphic card and or the chipset, could be expensive and for this reason I don't suggest any swap in this case. (unless they aren't working or if it's a brand new pc).

Another reason that I have to mention, is that swapping an HDD and the ram is a really easy task and if you aren't a service technician you can easily proceed without the risk of damaging your precious pc.

To clone your HDD, I would kindly suggest "Acronis" software that is really great.

Alternatively, you can use "EaseUS" that is another great tool.

Not only will help you to clone your HDD, but has some other great features.

Another thing you can do is add a secondary HDD (I would suggest a SSD of 250GB to run the operating system, and secondary HDD to store data (Es. 1 or 2 TB).

Acronis Vs. EaseUS

I prefer not to indicate any download links, as the internet world changes very quickly and any link indicated today may not work later on.

Just do a google search to get the correct download/purchase link.

As mentioned earlier, thay are both great products.

However, if for example you need to replace a 500GB HDD (with 80GB of data inside) with a smaller 250GB one, I recommend using EaseUS since Acronis unfortunately detects a smaller target HDD and could cause trouble.

Viceversa, EaseUS allows you to proceed smoothly even if the target HDD is smaller than the source one.

...and last but not least, Macrium Reflect

There is another interesting software called "Macrium Reflect", you can successfully use to clone your HDD, or to install your system image in your brand new laptop/desktop. (the laptop I used for this test, was equipped with M.2 SSD)

Chapter III
How to create an image recovery

I highly suggest to create an image recovery after you've installed the OS and have "tailored the machine" with software and apps to have a backup copy of the OS with all the program and tools you/your company needs, in order to recover faster a faulting pc or to install several new pc's.

Let's check together how to proceed with "Macrium Reflect".

After launching the program, just click as showed below: (as you can see, the HDD with the OS is already flagged)

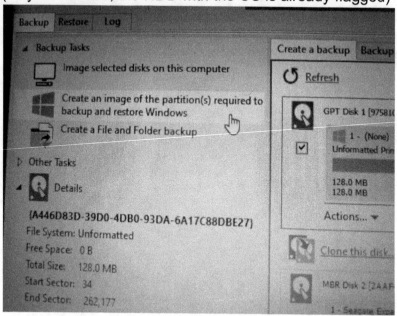

Next step, you need to select the image destination:

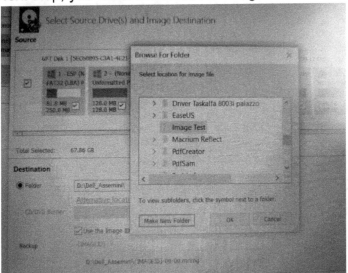

Then, after clicking ok, proceed with next:

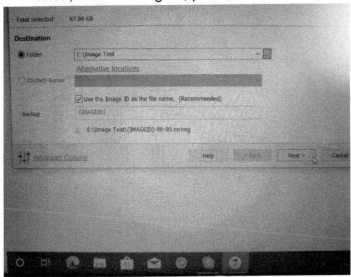

…again next…

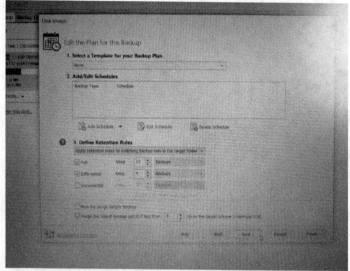

…click next after the summary…

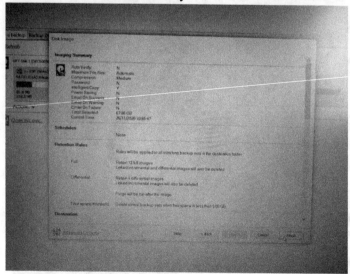

After clicking ok in this section…

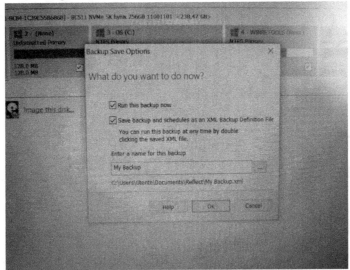

…the image creation will finally start…!

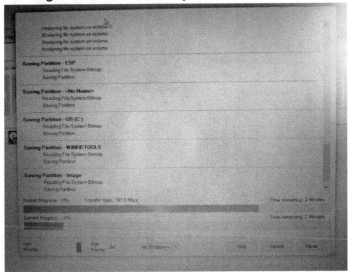

...after some minutes, the image will be complete!

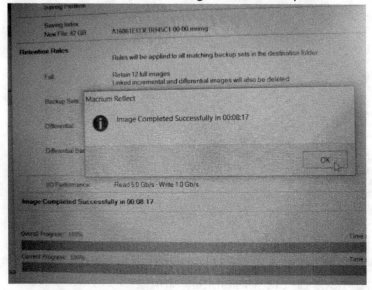

Installing from an image

Let's assume that you're the local IT of a company and your boss just asked you to prepare some brand new laptops (50) for a customer.

Let's see the procedure step by step.
You'll need a pendrive (better if usb 3.0), an external usb HDD or an SSD plugged into a docking station (up to usb 3.0) with the system image like the example below.

First of all, you'll need to configure the boot sequence from your pc's bios (please check manufacturer specs to verify the "boot key" to hold down at startup).

Moving on top of the list "USB DISK 3.0", you'll be able to to boot from the usb pendrive (where you previously installed Macrium Reflect or another one software mentioned earlier).

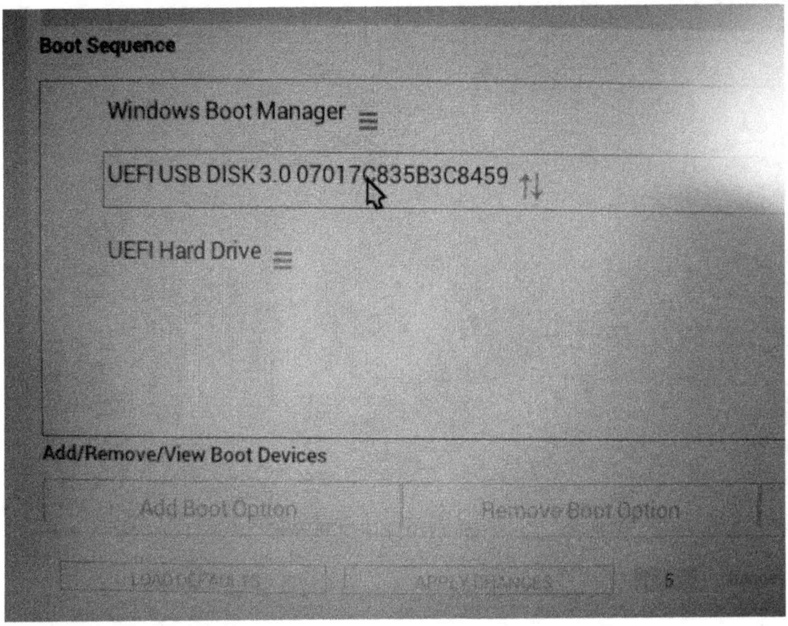

Boot Sequence

Windows Boot Manager ≡

UEFI USB DISK 3.0 07017C835B3C8459 ↑↓

UEFI Hard Drive ≡

Add/Remove/View Boot Devices

Add Boot Option   Remove Boot Option

LOAD DEFAULTS   APPLY CHANGES   5

Then you'll need to apply for the changes and restart your pc.

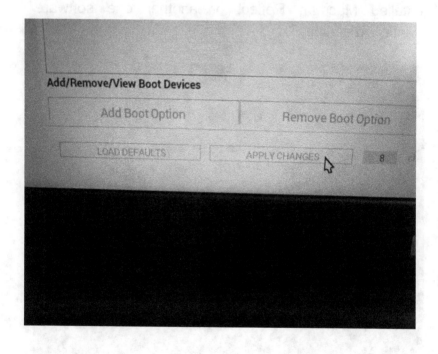

During restart you'll see something like this:

Then, you'll browse for the image location located in the external HDD;

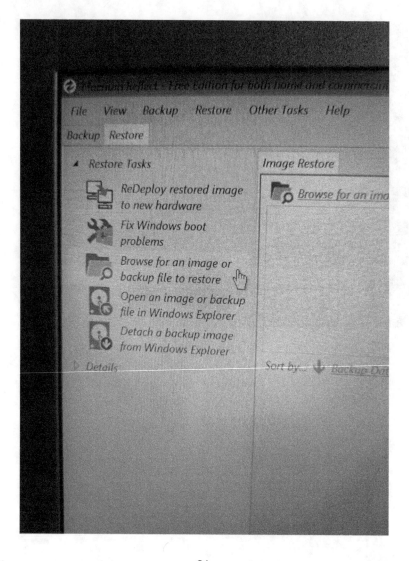

In the next menu, you'll select the exact location of the image:

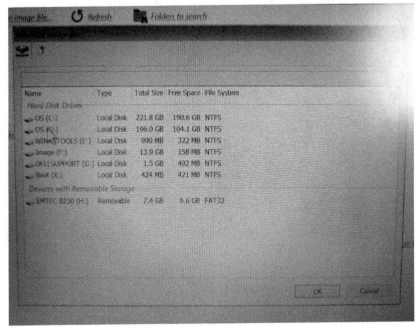

Pic. 1.1

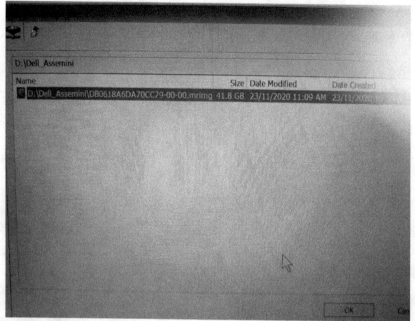

Pic. 2.2

And click ok, to confirm.

Then you'll click the "Restore Image" link:

So your image file, will be selected as "Source":

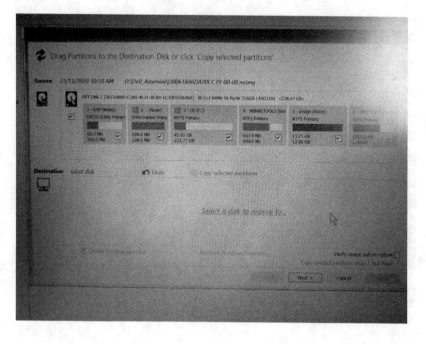

And, at this point you'll need to indicate the destination to restore the image...

Indicating the disk "C:" as destination.

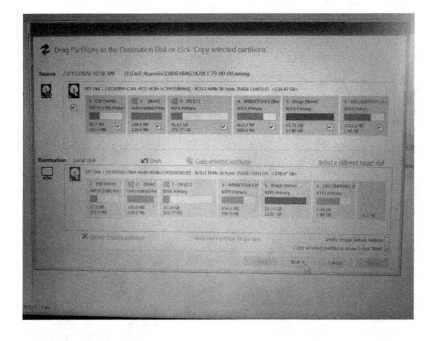

After confirming the "Restore summary" and another "warning overwrite confirming" (in the next page), the installation will start.

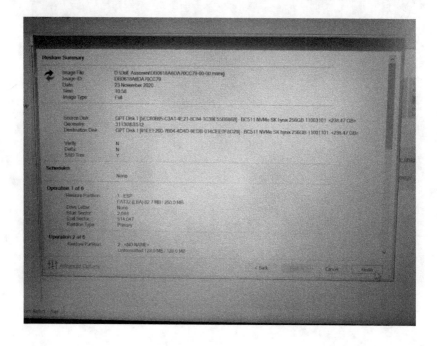

Demounting drives

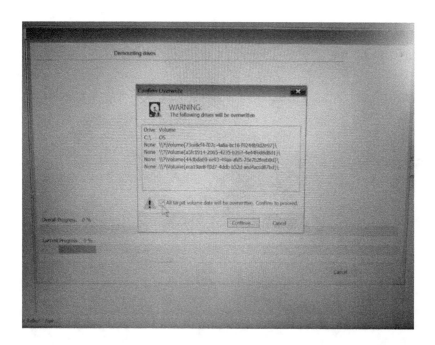

Confirm Overwrite

WARNING
The following drives will be overwritten

Drive Volume
C:\   OS
None   \\?\Volume{73ce8cf4-f07c-4a8a-bc16-f024db9d2e97}\
None   \\?\Volume{a5fc1914-2065-4235-b267-4e44f608d8d1}\
None   \\?\Volume{44dbda69-ee93-49aa-afd5-76e7b2feeb0d}\
None   \\?\Volume{eca19ac8-f0d7-4ddb-b52d-ae54accd87bd}\

All target volume data will be overwritten. Confirm to proceed.

Continue   Cancel

Overall Progress: 0 %

Current Progress: 0 %

Cancel

Restore timing, will depend by the source
performances…

Around 6 minutes (circa) with SSD "via docking station
usb 3.0":

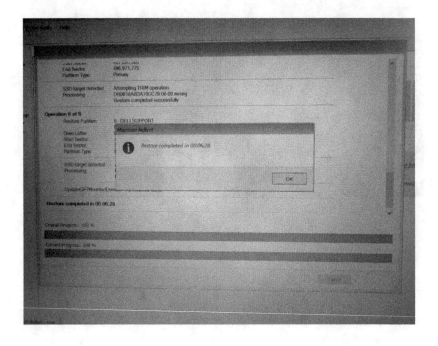

…or 51 minutes circa, via external HDD USB 2.0 as
shown in this picture:

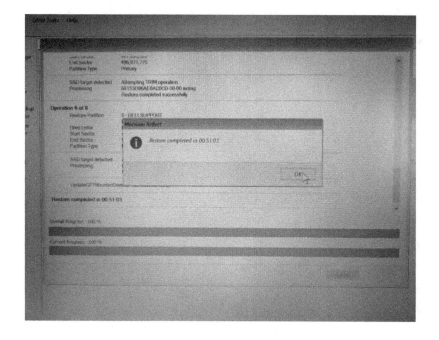

After removing the pendrive and the external HDD,
proceed with the system reboot.

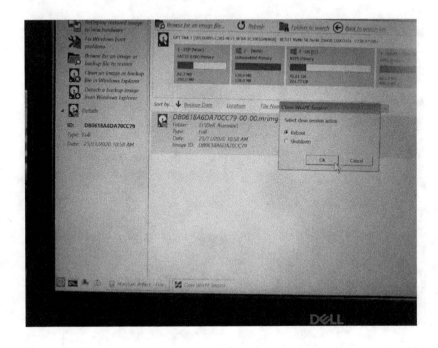

The laptop used in this test, started to update the firmware after reboot... so be aware to avoid power outages in order to don't damage your laptpop!

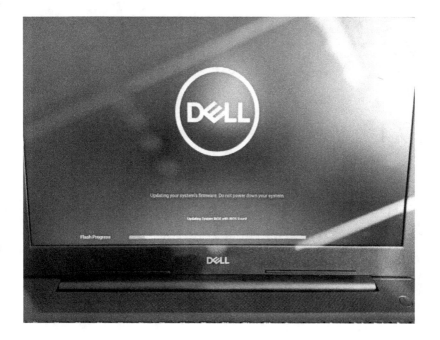

Before completing the firmware update, the laptop could reboot a couple of times… so don't worry and be ready to enjoy your brand new computer!

Chapter IV
Cloning HDD with Acronis

IMPORTANT: the cloned HDD will work in the same computer, or in a different one but with same hardware configuration.

Let's start connecting both HDD to the computer (The old one and the new SSD one).
If the computer shouldn't recognize the new HDD, check how to initialize and formatting a new HDD (later on, in this book).

You'll connect the new HDD with SATA and Power cable.

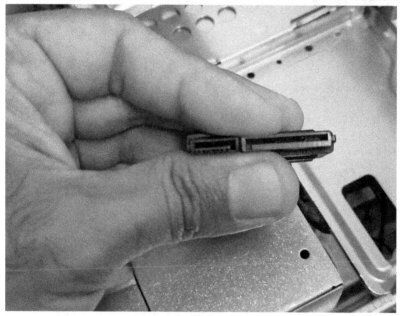

If you are using a bootable media with Acronis (Pendrive USB or CD/DVD), you need to arrange the boot options from the BIOS of your pc (please check the "BIOS key" to hold down when starting your computer).

When ready, select the "Primary boot sequence" from the Startup tab as showed below.

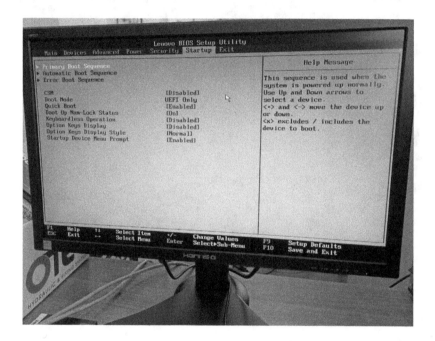

Then put on top of the list, the media you're using in order to make it the first boot device (in this case USB, since I used a pendrive).

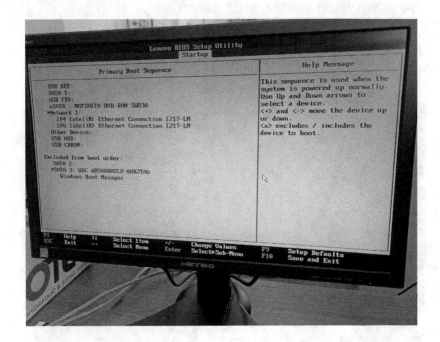

Then, choose "Save and exit" option to reboot from usb (in this case F10 key).

During reboot you'll see Acronis loading...

Then click on Acronis True Image

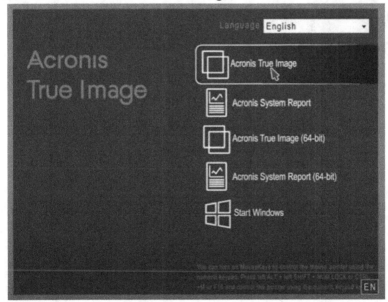

Click "Clone Disk" on the "Tools & Utilities" tab on the home screen.

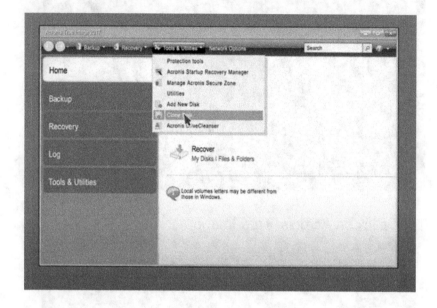

Select clone mode, and click Next as showed below.

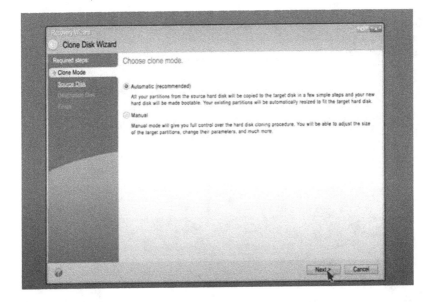

Select the source disk and click next.

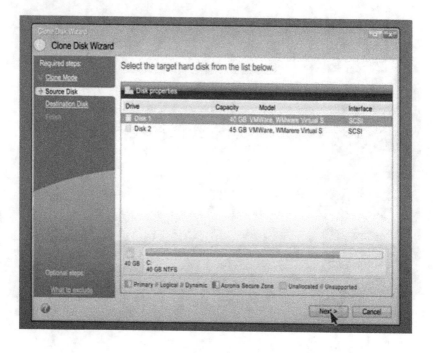

Select the destination disk and click next.

In the summary screen, do a last check and if everything is ok click proceed.

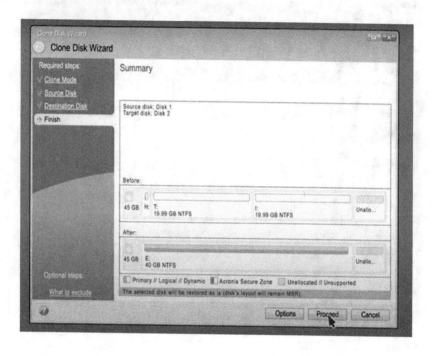

Acronis will start cloning the old disk to the new disk, indicating the progress. You can choose if restart or shutdown the computer at the end of the task.

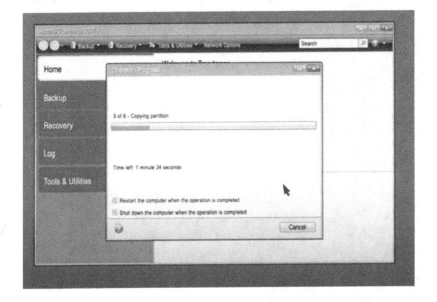

After the cloning operation is complete, you'll see the end message.

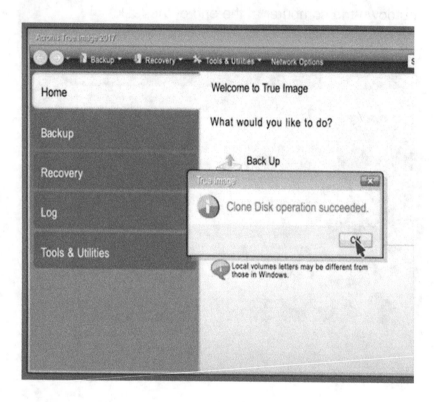

IMPORTANT: remember to disconnect the old HDD from the computer and arrange again the boot options from the BIOS.

Initializing and formatting a new HDD in Windows 10

Let's move on to see how to prepare the brand new HDD.

Right click on start menu, and then click on "Disk Management" as showed below:

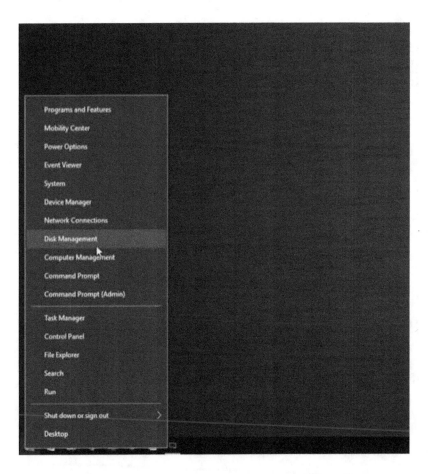

This is a really important task, because if you don't format the new HDD, will doesn't show up in Windows (despite being phisically connected to the pc).

Disk Management will pop up, asking how do you want to initialize it:

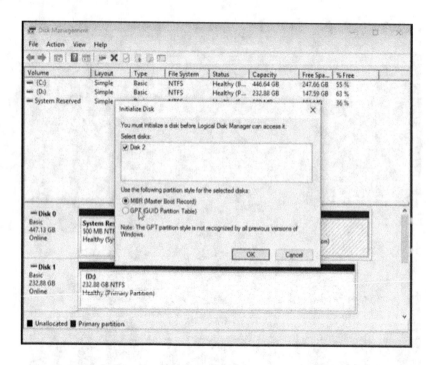

If your drive is up to 2TB, you can choose MBR as showed in the above picture.

If you have a drive larger than 2TB, choose GPT:

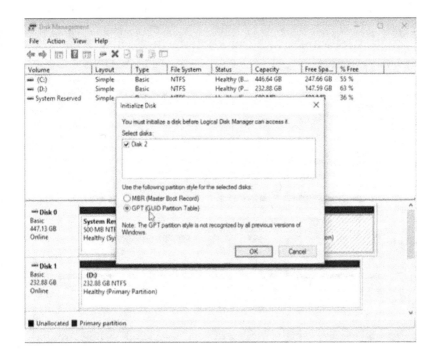

IMPORTANT: MBR works with every version of Windows, but don't works with drive larger than 2TB.

GPT works with drive larger than 2 TB but not with all Windows versions.

Since this drive is smaller than 2TB, I choose MBR.

Now you can see the new drive (Disk 2) as showed below.

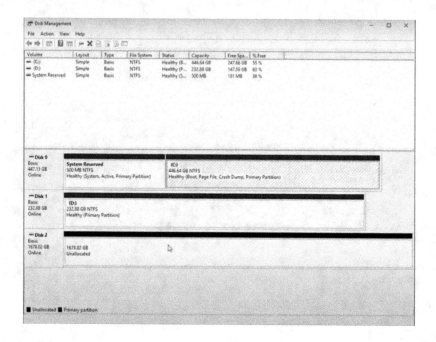

Right click on Drive 2 and then click "New simple volume".

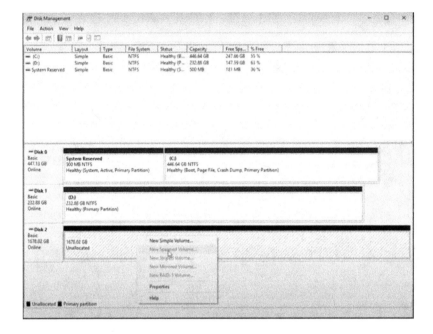

Then, click next when "New simple volume wizard" pops up.

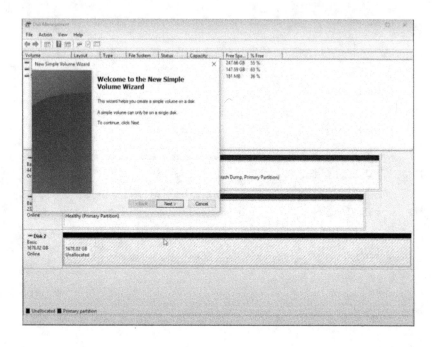

Leave default option and click next.

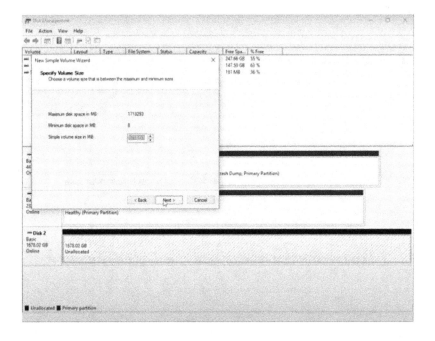

I recommend to leave default drive letter, the other options and click next.

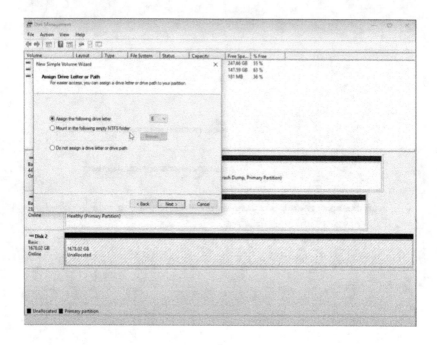

You can leave the default options or if you want, you can delete the "Volume label" and leave it empty.

Leave enabled as showed below "Perform a quick format", because otherwise it could take a very long time.

Do not enable file and folder compression.

Then, click next.

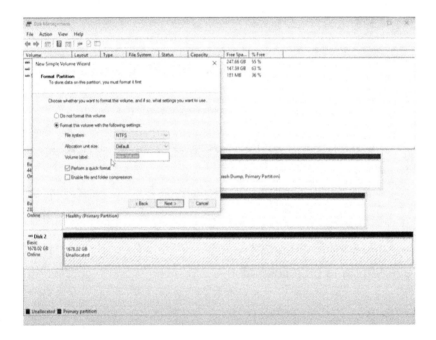

The next step, will show the summary of the chosed details.

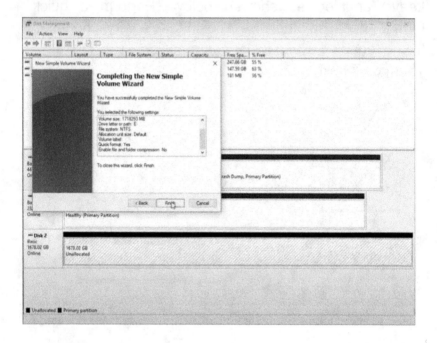

If everything is ok, click finish.

The click on format disk.

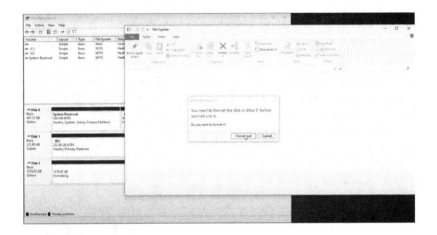

Then will start formatting…

After a couple of seconds… or more (depending on the performances of your pc), your drive will be ready.

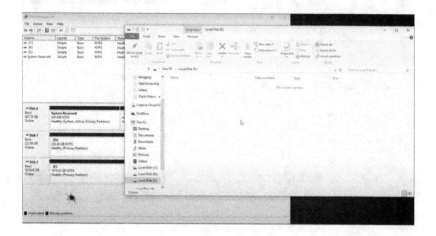

If you click on "this pc", you'll see the new drive "E:"

Chapter V
About RAM

You might think that Windows PCs have more than enough memory.

Even budget systems come with at least 4GB, and you can add 4GB spending little money.

Surely 8GB should be enough, right?

Well... maybe not.

You can very quickly find that your 4GB system is grinding to a halt thanks to hungry applications.

Let's check some memory basics...

Most 32-bit Windows systems can address a maximum of 3.12GB RAM.

This isn't the CPU's fault, in fact modern processors have a 36-bit address mode that allows them to access up to 64GB of ram.

Programs have to be aware of these 36-bit addresses, though, if not, they'll truncate them to 32-bit and read/write data in the wrong place.

That's one reason why Microsoft restricted all 32-bit client versions of Windows to a maximum 4GB of RAM.

That's one reason why Microsoft restricted all 32-bit client versions of Windows to a maximum 4GB of RAM.

That 4GB address space is split into two.

Windows and your drivers get 2GB to themselves, and Windows fools each of your applications into thinking that it has sole access to the other 2GB.

You could have five programs running at the same time, each using between 1GB and 2GB of memory, so the 4GB figure isn't quite the limit it seems at first.

Memory is allocated in units called page, usually 4KB in size, which are tracked in the PFN (Page Frame Number) database.

If you have 2GB or RAM but your programs need to use 3GB, Windows will find pages in physical memory that haven't been accessed recently and write them to a paging file on your hard drive.

The physical RAM is then freed up for use by the latest program you're running.

This mechanism lets you bypass the 4GB address space limit and run many more applications, but there is a price to pay for it.

It takes much longer to access an HDD than actual RAM, and so the more use that's made of your paging file, the slower your system will get.

Upgrading memory (RAM)

Another way to improve performances, is upgrading the ram.
Before proceeding, you must check the motherboard specs in order to see how much ram can support.
Let's check for example the following motherboard:

If you google "ASUS P8H67-M", you'll find that supports a maximum amount of ram of 32GB.

It's equipped with four slots for the ram modules, so you'll put four modules of 8GB.

This is a check that must be carried out each time you want to increase the ram on a pc.

RICCARDO RUGGIU was born in Cagliari in 1976. He works in the silicon-based technology sector from over twenty years, and developed a deep experience working for the largest and major IT companies in Italy and abroad.

After publishing "Stupidario tecnico: 101 frasi dette dai clienti all'Help Desk", "How to look for and get a job" and "How to buy High Fidelity", has devoted himself to writing this manual for improving and/or restoring pc's performances.

Riccardo would love to hear about your experiences with this book (the good, the bad, and the ugly).
You can write to him at:
ultimateguideforspeedupyourpc@gmail.com.

www.ingramcontent.com/pod-product-compliance
Lightning Source LLC
LaVergne TN
LVHW051747050326
832903LV00029B/2769

* 9 7 9 8 5 7 4 0 8 5 9 0 5 *